D0875557

The American Journalists

AMERICAN JOURNALISM

Henry King

ARNO
&
The New York Times

Collection Created and Selected

by Charles Gregg of Gregg Press

Reprint edition 1970 by Arno Press Inc.

LC# 79-125700
ISBN 0-405-01679-4

The American Journalists
ISBN for complete set: 0-405-01650-6

Reprinted from a copy in
The Kansas State Historical Society Library

Manufactured in the United States of America

AMERICAN JOURNALISM.

ADDRESS

OF

CAPT. HENRY KING,

DELIVERED BEFORE THE EDITORS' AND PUBLISHERS' ASSOCIATION OF
KANSAS, AT FRAZER'S HALL, LAWRENCE, TUESDAY
EVENING, OCTOBER 24TH, 1871.

To which is Appended a

REPORT OF THE PROCEEDINGS

OF THE

SIXTH ANNUAL CONVENTION

OF THE

Kansas Editors and Publishers' Association,

HELD AT LAWRENCE

OCTOBER 24TH AND 25TH, 1871.

TOPEKA, KANSAS:
PRINTED AT THE COMMONWEALTH STATE PRINTING HOUSE.
1871.

ADDRESS:

Tradition tells us that in the olden time the reapers always left untouched the corners of the fields, so that the poor gleaners who came behind them might secure grain enough to pay them for their toil. The very excellent reapers who have preceded me in the field I am expected to traverse to-night have done such thorough work that gleaning after them seems a task of doubtful profit. Still, they may have left a little something worth gathering and garnering. Bespeaking your indulgence, I will make the search and see what I can find.

THE COLONIAL PAPERS.

In all the precious freight of the *Mayflower* there was not a single printing-press. The first one was brought over from England eighteen years after the Pilgrims landed. An attempt was made to establish a weekly newspaper in 1690, but the authorities allowed only one number to be issued. Fourteen years later a second and successful venture was made by John Campbell, the postmaster at Boston. He called his paper the Boston

News Letter. It was printed on one side of a sheet of foolscap, and its news from Europe was five months old. A rival paper, called the Boston *Gazette*, was started in 1719 by a new postmaster who superseded Campbell—and post-offices have somehow had an attraction for editors ever since, though I regret to say they don't always get them when they ask for them. In 1721 James Franklin established his *New England Courant*, a decided improvement on the other papers then being published. Very soon, however, it got into trouble with the clergy on the exciting issue of inoculation; and the Colonial government retired the publisher from business and furnished him quarters and subsistence at the public expense. Franklin's brother, Ben, then an apprentice in his teens, succeeded to the control of the *Courant*, and there gained much of the tact and wisdom which he subsequently put to such extensive and profitable use on the *Gazette* at Philadelphia, the first really creditable newspaper published in North America. The *Gazette* was merely a newspaper, however, and although for a long time the leading journal of the Continent, its editorials, when it had any, rarely touched political topics. Questions of grave import were then discussed in communications, or in pamphlets, after the English method.

THE FIRST POLITICAL JOURNAL.

Not until 1733, nearly a century after the first printing materials reached the country, did a political journal proper make its appearance. It was a "campaign" paper called the *Weekly Journal*, started at New York by John Peter Zenger to oppose the Colonial administration of Governor Crosby. The government instituted a libel suit against Zenger, who, after a long and exciting trial was acquitted, amid the applause of the spectators; and the municipal authorities voted the freedom of the city and a magnificent gold snuff box to his eminent counsel, Andrew Hamilton, "for the remarkable service done to the inhabitants of the Colony by his defense of the rights of mankind and the liberty of the press." Bancroft says that a patriot of the time esteemed this trial to have been " the morning-star of the American Revolution." It disenthralled and emboldened the whole Colonial press, and made it a conspicuous and powerful agency in preparing the way for independence.

THE PRESS FROM 1776 TO 1800.

At the commencement of the Revolution the Colonies had thirty-seven papers, all weekly but one, the Philadelphia *Advertiser*, which was published twice a week. The war gave birth to a number of new papers; and in the year following its close the first daily—the Philadelphia *Packet*—was established. In the early part of Washington's administration, two opposition political "organs" were started, one controlled by Hamilton and Adams, the other by Madison and Jefferson. These papers inaugurated the first newspaper war under the Republic, and it raged for eight years with all the fury of a " purification" contest in Kansas.

When Adams became President, in 1797, he found almost the whole press of the country opposed to him. The next year the administration party armed itself with the sedition law, and sallied forth to crush what it could not control. The effort was a failure. The papers, backed by the people, were too strong to be put down; and the Federal party found itself, like another Milo, wedged in the timber which it had vainly striven to rend. Adams was beaten for re-election by over a two-thirds vote, and the opposition put in his place Thomas Jefferson, who declared he would rather live in a country with newspapers and without a government, than in a country with a government and without newspapers.

NEWSPAPER PROGRESS SINCE 1800.

Under Jefferson the press was loosed from all governmental bonds, and sent forth to seek its fortune in its own way. How completely and how splendidly it has justified the faith that gave it a free field of effort let the faith that gave it a free field of effort let the record of the last seventy years stand witness. Year by year there has been a steady growth in the number and excellence of all kinds of newspapers. From two hundred at the beginning of the century, they have increased to nearly five thousand, with an aggregate circulation little short of fifteen hundred million copies; and they wield a power more potent than the combined influence of all the other instrumentalities now at work in the land. They build up, and they pull down, at their royal pleasure—moulding policies, producing reforms, anticipating statesmanship, giving history its flexure and its force. Joining the functions of the essayist with those of the news-vender, our journalism has created a new profession and fashioned a new form of literature. The editor, once considered little better than a vagabond, has become the monarch of popular opinion; and his calling, once classed with those of the chimney-sweep and scissors-grinder, has been exalted to a place among the most reputable and important of human pursuits. Compare the newspapers of 1800 with those of the succeeding years, down to the present, and you will see each step of our growth and improvement as a nation and a people; for the history of the United States, in the highest sense, is but the history of its press—the story of bold hearts and clear heads making the types wage ceaseless warfare against error and fraud with stout English words—

" Wherein Truth's utterances, sandaled and shod,
Have marched down the age for Freedom and God."

THE JOURNALISM OF TO-DAY.

The journalism of the period—the current newspaper style, so to speak—is the outgrowth of the last fifteen years. The memorable struggle in Kansas furnished the occasion and the materials for its origination, and the necessities of the terrible war that followed gave it development. It is altogether American; and its vantage ground is "the living present." It is not perfect, of course; but it has attained a degree of excellence that surpasses all competition in other countries, and manifested a capacity for improvement that promises it a future of increased and incalculable power, prosperity and usefulness.

The demand upon editors and publishers for good work has never before been so general and so pressing as it is just now. The sphere of their efforts has been so greatly enlarged, and the appliances at their command so amply augmented, that their patrons will not and should not tolerate careless or stupid labor at their hands. To pilot a newspaper in these days requires a quick eye and a steady hand. The public taste must be consulted and satisfied, or there can be no success. And the public taste that we have now to deal with is as different from that of fifteen years ago as the present condition of the country—materially, morally and politically—is unlike that which existed when the Kansas pioneers "staked out" their first "claims."

THE IMPORTANCE OF GOOD PRESS-WORK.

To secure attention and patronage, a newspaper should have, first of all, a clean face, and be clad in a comely garb. That is, its typographical appearance should be neat, tasty and attractive. There is no valid excuse at this time for publishing any other kind of paper. The art of printing has reached a stage that renders "black

smithing" not only disreputable, but unprofitable also.
It is easier and cheaper and more remunerative to make
a nice paper than a slovenly one. It requires only a
small assortment of good materials and a fair amount of
careful labor to produce a tidy and engaging sheet. Two
fonts of body type, a little display letter and a platen
press, in the hands of a printer who knows his business,
are sufficient for the performance of the work in a creditable manner.

Most depends upon the press-work. The handsomest
of type loses its beauty in an unclean "impression;" and
dirty work is as often done on cylinders as on the hand-
press Some of the best printing I have ever seen was
produced with platen presses; and there are papers
printed upon such presses in this State to-day that are
not excelled in appearance by the finest of our "cylinder"
journals. Good ink, good paper and good rollers are the
prime factors in the problem of good press-work. The
use of cheap ink or an inferior quality of paper is the
poorest of economy; and a printer who cannot make a
good roller or detect a bad one has never learned his
trade, no matter how high a place he may hold in the
Typographical Union.

The Kansas papers, I am proud to say, are, as a class,
models of excellence in this respect. No State in the
Union has better printed papers. Still, the handsomest
of them can be improved; and a few of them are shame-
fully shabby.

THE "MAKE-UP" OF A NEWSPAPER.

The "make-up" of a newspaper is next in importance
to the manner of its printing. I prefer an orderly dis-
tribution of reading matter over all the pages, or at least
over three of the four pages. Each kind of matter—as
news, miscellany, editorials, communications, local intel-

9

ligence, etc.—should always have its allotted and established place in the paper. Throwing in all forms of matter, here to-day and there to-morrow, without any regard to rule or fitness, confuses and vexes the reader and gives the paper an aspect of general shiftlessness.

The whole paper, too, should be "set up" and printed in the office from which it purports to come. "Patent outsides" are a fraud and an abomination: a half a paper is little, if any, better than no paper at all.

ABOUT SELECTIONS OF "COPY."

Selections of "copy" should be made with great care, preference always being given to that which will enlighten us well as entertain. The best test of editorship is in the making of selections. The writing of editorials is the smallest part of an industrious and conscientious editor's work. A hundred men can write well where one can make proper selections. Many of the most competent editors in the country, properly speaking, manufacture the lamest and dullest of "leaders," while on the other hand, many of our most brilliant writers, if placed in absolute charge of a paper, would prove failures inside of six months.

To make proper and pleasing selections requires a rare tact, a sort of sixth sense, which is acquired only in the school of experience. As a general rule, however, selections should be short, and pertain mainly to matters of current public interest. The mass of readers care but little for Belshazzar and Hector and Augustus; they want to know what "Boss" Tweed and Wild Bill and Brigham Young are about—how Grant is getting along with the public debt, and Bob Stevens with his railroad, and Andy Wilson with his cattle. When they feel like going back of such things, they buy books.

CONCERNING ADVERTISEMENTS.

Advertisements, like other kinds of newspaper matter, ought to be classified and put in a regular place. The style of this part of the paper, of course, depends largely upon the will of the advertisers, and yet the publishers can and should give it character and interest.

For over half a century after the origin of newspapers, no advertisements appeared, the practice then being to "fill up" the vacant space with a chapter or two from the Bible. Only within the last ten or twelve years, in fact, has advertising come to be regarded as a perfectly legitimate mode of seeking trade. Now, everybody advertises that expects to thrive—not simply because it is a prevailing custom, but chiefly because the custom itself is a paying one. Advertising has revolutionized our daily business, giving us new habits, new thoughts and new enterprises. The advertising columns of a modern newspaper are really the most valuable and interesting of its contents, and there is still abundant room to make them more so.

To my mind, what are called "standing" advertisements—that is, such as remain unchanged for six or twelve months—are almost worthless to the advertiser and a positive injury to the paper. It would be vastly better for all concerned, in my judgment, if advertisements were changed with each appearance. Such a method would compel attention and impart freshness to a portion of the paper that is now rarely read on account of its forbidding sameness. A few of our shrewdest advertisers understand this, and do most of their "blowing" by means of "local notices" inserted for one time only. If they were to extend the practice to the advertising columns proper they would find it correspondingly profitable—and I am sure no publisher would enter any objection.

Those "fearful and wonderful" cuts that illustrate many of our advertisements, I would have tossed into the "hell-box," where they properly belong. They disfigure a paper, and disgust a hundred persons where they favorably affect half a dozen. An intelligent man would have to be very sick, it strikes me, to buy a patent medicine commended to his attention through the medium of a picture representing an imaginary sea-monster in the act of swallowing a suppositious maiden afloat "all forlorn" on waves lashed into an impossible fury. Such caricatures might do for dime novels. But the class who read dime novels seldom purchase anything but chewing-gum and fine-tooth combs.

The people whose attention it is really desirable for the trader to attract can easiest and surest be reached, in my estimation, by modest and sensible advertisements, in small type and without pictures. Sensational advertising has had its day; and the men who still adhere to it are simply throwing away their money, to say nothing of making themselves appear ridiculous in the eyes of all intelligent readers.

GIVING THE NEWS.

"A daily paper," observes philosopher Goodwin, of the Sedalia Bazoo, "is a paper which is published every day." So, I may say, the foremost function of a newspaper, as its name implies, is to give the news. The news, in this day signifies, in full reality,

"A map of busy life—
Its fluctuations, and its vast concerns,"

throughout the globe. At the touch of the telegraph the whole world has become 'kin. Yesterday's doings in all the capitals of the Eastern Hemisphere are spread before us in this morning's papers, fresh as the news from Washington. And the railroad has furnished us with mails that pass from ocean to ocean in five days, putting

New York and San Francisco in closer connection than existed fifteen years ago between Lawrence and St. Louis. Marvelous, indeed, are the triumphs which the wire and the engine have wrought over time and space, within the memory of the youngest of us—triumphs well worth glorifying, too, if it did take lands and bonds to bring them.

The present American system of collecting and publishing news has sprung out of our necessities as a people. There is nothing rivaling it in extent and vigor anywhere else in the world The European papers do not furnish a tenth part as much real news, domestic or foreign, as do those of this country. Their telegrams are brief and unimportant; their correspondence, save in war time, is hardly worth mentioning; and their local intelligence is confined almost exclusively to weather reports, royal personals and court receptions. Last May, a convention of six hundred ministers sat for days in London discussing questions that affected the very stability of the government, and the *Times* gave not a word of their proceedings. And Senator Wilson relates that during his recent visit to the same city, there was a meeting of the Royal Geographical Society, at which the Emperor of Brazil made a set speech, and none of the next morning's papers devoted over an inch of space to the important affair. How differently we do such things in the United States nobody needs to be told.

OUR ASSOCIATED PRESS DISPATCHES.

Seventy years ago, it took twenty days to get the most important news from Paris to London, and twice as much longer to bring it to America. Even forty years ago, it required twelve and one-half hours to pass the President's message from New York to Boston: last December a similar document was transmitted over the ten telegraph

wires between Washington and New York in a little
more than sixty minutes.

Our telegraphic news reports, as we now get them,
are of comparatively recent origin. The Associated
Press, that mightiest of modern co-operative enterprises,
was not organized until 18⁵8, and the first extensive
employment of the wires for news purposes was by the
Chicago papers during the Lincoln—Douglas campaign
of that year, in Illinois. The war made full and regular
news dispatches a permanent and indispensable feature
of our journalism; and newspaper readers have come to
expect them as naturally as they look for the sunrise.
That these reports are always reliable and never " colored"
to serve partisan or personal ends, cannot, in truth, be
said. But that they meet an important popular want,
and that, sensational as they sometimes are, it would be
almost impossible to " keep house" without them, nobody
will deny.

THE LOCAL DEPARTMENT OF A PAPER.

The telegraphic reports, however, form only one divi-
sion of the news system. Still more important and interesting to most readers than the movements of Kings and
Presidents, than the condition of affairs in Paris or the
new developments of roguery in that modern Sodom
where Tammany rules and robs, are the daily occurrences
of a local character. Home news should be first and most
sedulously sought. No amount or quality of outside intelligence, of selected matter, or of editorial sharp shoot-
ing will atone for a lack of attention to local affairs.
Every community likes to be kept posted on what is
transpiring in its own midst. Nine out of every ten
readers habitually turn to the local page of a paper and
devour its contents greedily, reading the rest of the sheet
at their leisure. Their uppermost wish, naturally enough,

is to learn how things are running at home—what accidents have happened; who of the townsfolk have died, got married, eloped or gone visiting; when the mite societies are to hold their next meetings; what brute of a husband has been blacking his wife's eye, or what medal deserving woman has broom-sticked her drunken husband; when the next excursion is to take place; who has paid tribute to the police magistrate; what stores are selling off at cost; and the scores of other things that the people talk of and think about amid the rush and bustle of every-day life. A good local reporter who industriously looks after these matters and serves them up in an agreeable style is worth three times as much to a paper as the amount of his salary ever indicates.

THE COUNTRY PAPERS' BEST FIELD.

In the department of local affairs the country papers have a field that they should till with the utmost industry. Few of them give it half the attention it deserves. A weekly paper will gain higher standing, both at home and abroad, by devoting all its "leaded" space to town and county matters than by passing such things to discuss abstruse political problems or wage a high-toned war against the moral and social evils that afflict modern society.

The dearth of news, and the difficulties of finding local items, that country papers—and city papers, too, for that matter—so frequently whine about are purely imaginary. The materials are always plentiful. The fact that no murder has been committed in the town during the week doesn't signify that other things of quite as much general interest have not happened. Five hundred people cannot live in a town together for seven days without making enough local history to fill at least one page of a seven-column paper. The courts, the schools and the churches, the traders, the mechanics and the mischief-makers, are always doing something worth telling.

A lazy and incompetent editor is continually chiding his readers about their duty to their home paper, while the editor who really understands his business seeks favor and patronage by furnishing a paper that the public cannot do without. To make a good paper, a paper whose constant excellence shall command attention and respect, is the true secret of successful journalism. No other theory will win, no matter how much scolding may be done, or how many sewing-machines and galvanized watches may be given away as premiums.

LOCAL JOB-PRINTING.

Right here, a few words about local job-printing. A great many suppose, or seem to suppose, that when they subscribe for and advertise in their local papers they do all that may rightfully be expected of them. This is a radical error. A man wrongs and cripples his home press whenever he sends away for any sort of printing that can be obtained in his own town. Whatever work the local printer can do in the line of his art the community ought to give him, cheerfully and without solicitation, even though he may sometimes be unable to duplicate metropolitan prices. All our railroads, banks, insurance companies, merchants and public officials should have their printing done at home. Not only are they in equity bound to do so, but they will, considering everything, find it also the more profitable course to pursue. Thousands of dollars are annually sent out of this State for printing which ought all to be given to our own offices—printing that can nearly always be as finely and cheaply done here as anywhere in the country. The Kansas press richly deserves every dollar's worth of work that Kansas communities have to give; and the man who sends east

for his cards, letter-heads, handbills, blank books, etc.,
ought to be ashamed to look his local printer in the face.

CORRESPONDENCE, REGULAR AND VOLUNTARY.

Correspondence, regular and voluntary, forms an
important part of all good newspapers. This feature is
the oldest in journalism—older than advertisements, editorials or news reports. Franklin used it in this country
when our press was in its infancy; the ablest statesmen
of the period wrote for the Colonial journals; Alexander
Hamilton commenced his remarkable career as a newspaper contributor; and the first "official organ" under
the Federal government—Fenno's New York *Gazette*—
had John Adams for a correspondent. It has been but
a short time, however, since our correspondents, as such,
became a separate guild and power. The profession as
it now exists was founded here in Kansas, and Phillips,
Redpath and Hinton were its prophets. During the great
rebellion the correspondents rendered services of signal
value, and they are to-day giving us some of the keenest
and strongest of our writing. That they occasionally
deal in sensations must be confessed; but their sinning
in that respect is a thousand times atoned by the truths
they tell us.

But newspaper correspondence should not be confined
to the letters of professional writers. It should include
contributions from all sources and on all topics of interest.
Most editors do not know the real value of correspondence and do not treat it with proper attention. Private
observers can often present a favorite subject in a more
striking and satisfactory manner than the best of editors.
A column communication from an anonymous writer, a
few years ago, changed the public opinion of half New
England on a vital financial issue. And the best article
ever published in Kansas on the woman question was

contributed to a Topeka paper last winter by a lady who
modestly declined to furnish her name.

The columns of public journals ought be thrown open
without partiality or reserve to contributions of all kinds
—to discussions of important questions, descriptions of
towns and their business, reports of farming operations,
accounts of neighborhood meetings, and so on. Let the
people talk to one another through your papers : it will
please them and profit you. Invite and urge them to
print their views on matters of local political concern,
and to send you news items of every sort. No other kind
of matter that you can publish will make your papers
more sought after by all classes of readers or win for
them more favor from the best of advertisers.

EDITORIAL WRITING.

The editorial writing that "takes" and is effective in
this country at the present time owns no model and was
shaped after no definite rule. Like Topsey, it "jest
growed." Twenty years ago, first class editorials were
as long as latter-day magazine articles, and as dry as a list
of advertised letters. The editor of that era was a man
of many words, and those the biggest he could find. He
doted on Dr. Johnson, and learned quotations were the
delight of his soul. To be profoundly flat was apparently
his controlling aim; and men read his ponderous screeds
with sacramental solemnity. The improvements in printing, the rapid extension of railroads, and the employment
of the telegraph as a news-carrier, gradually shortened
and gave pith and plainness to newspaper talking. The
Fremont canvass, the Kansas struggle, and the campaign
of 1860, had each its new and peculiar editorial dialect;
and each was better, braver and brighter than the fashion
which it superseded. When the war came, with its terrible awakening of energy, its rush and roar of furious

2

elements, still another advance became necessary: the ancient prophecy was reversed, and the pen that the fogies had used as a plough-share was changed to a sword, which cut as never sword had cut before. The tread of armies and the shock of battle called for "short, sharp and decisive" editorials, that should strike the brain like a bullet. And when peace returned, our journalism required no Fifteenth Amendment to fasten its progress; its emancipation from the follies and stupidities of past times was already a fixed fact—and it has been getting further and further away from them ever since.

BREVITY AND PLAINNESS DEMANDED.

The editor who expects to be listened to in these days must, first of all, learn to express his thoughts and views in the fewest and plainest of words. Our people have neither time nor patience to sit still and be pumped into by the column. They want brief and pungent writing that goes straight to the heart of the theme. " The force of style," says our greatest prose-writer, " consists in striking out." A single paragraph of half a dozen pointed sentences will command closer attention and prove more effective than an article twenty times as long, in which the same ideas are elaborated with artistic minuteness. " In firing at a bird," once said an eminent orator, " it is useless to take aim at each feather separately; bring down the bird and the feathers will come too."

A very good article can be written with a very economical use of the dictionary. Our language contains about a hundred thousand words; but it is not necessary to use the whole number on a newspaper. Three-fourths of them, in fact, are " all Dutch" to the average reader. Most persons of fair intelligence are not familiar with more than four thousand; our best living writers and

speakers rarely employ as high as ten thousand; Milton
used only eight thousand; and Shakspeare himself, who
explored the whole realm of human thought, found
fifteen thousand quite as many as he needed.

Take the great Eastern dailies, and if you have never
noticed it before, you will be surprised at finding what
ordinary words and what homely illustrations they use,
even on the most weighty of topics. They do so because
such a style is easiest understood and appreciated, and
therefore most effective. It is not quantity that tells, but
quality; and the editor who cannot resist the inclination
to "slop over," as we term it, had better turn auctioneer
or go to dealing in patent rights. Journalism has no use
for him.

PERSONALITIES.

I am aware that brief and pungent writing is apt to
run into personalities. That is the main reason why I
commend it. I believe in personalities. The journalist is
never so powerful as when he is personal. To proclaim
truth in a general way is well; but to give it personal appli-
cation is immeasurably better. Archbishop Whately once
said he believed people should go to church to be made
uncomfortable. And I hold, on the same ground, that a
newspaper is a failure which does not make bad men
squirm whenever they read it. Denouncing knavery in
the abstract is like tossing pebbles into an ocean; it is only
when scoundrels are specifically collared and held up to
public scorn and scoffing that the waters are "troubled"
to some purpose. Nathan preached general principles
to David at first, in the form of a parable; but the guilty
monarch sat unmoved until the prophet pointed a finger
in his face and said "Thou art the man!"

Over a century ago the personalities of "Junius"
brought fear and trembling to the King, Lords and Com-
mons of Great Britain; and Franklin, Hamilton and

their co-workers employed the same weapon with good effect in early American times. The best political writers, the most influential editors, have always been exceedingly, and often offensively, personal in their criticisms. Take the personalities out of our journalism, and it would go into bankruptcy. Banish the words blackguard, liar and villain from our newspaper literature, and even the "good and useful" Greeley would quit the business in disgust. Personalities are to true and forcible journalism what the orthodox old lady declared total depravity was to her system of faith and worship: "Why take away my total depravity," said she, "and you take away my religion!" Deny the journalist the privilege of attacking rascals and tricksters by name, and you deprive his profession of the very element that most makes it a power for good in the land.

TOO MANY PAPERS IN KANSAS.

I would not be understood as favoring personal contests between editors, although even they are preferable, I think, to a total lack of energetic and spicy writing. In fact, I do not see how we could well get along without them here in Kansas We have so many papers and such sharp rivalry that occasional clashings are not easily to be avoided. The truth is, the number of our papers is nearly twice as large as it ought to be. There are at least a score and a half of editors and publishers in this State who would do both themselves and the profession a profitable service by going to farming or stock-raising. Not that they are specially unfitted for journalism, but because the business is overdone, and the competition is so close that living profits are out of the question—and the profits, after all, are of first importance.

The evil is intensified by the fact that on account of the Democratic party making such poor headway in this

section, our papers are mostly Republican in politics.
Two papers of the same politics published in the same
town, unless it be quite a large one, are almost uni-
formly at swords' points with each other. By underbid-
ding on municipal and county work, they render it prac-
tically valueless; and a standard scale of prices for private printing and advertising is not adhered to by either
of them if the other can in any instance be beaten by
ignoring it. Worse than this, they produce party dis-
cord, create cliques and engender petty local spites and
wranglings. Each paper naturally has its coterie of
admirers and champions; and whatever one advocates
or recommends the other ridicules and opposes, as a matter of course. I need not cite examples. Most of you
" know how it is yourselves."

The number of daily papers in Kansas ought to be
reduced, by consolidation or otherwise, at least one-half,
and the weekly papers fully one-third, if not more. No
one of our cities, with the exception of Leavenworth,
needs more than one daily; and very few of the interior
towns should have more than one weekly each. If such
a reduction as I suggest could be made, we would have
better papers, the printing business would be worth following, and personal contests between rival editors would
become rare enough to be really enjoyable.

INDEPENDENCE.

The course of the press as a public instructor and
reformer is necessarily subject, in some degree, to the
control of circumstances. New occasions create new
duties and demand new tactics. In general outline,
however, the policy of the conscientious journalist is
inflexible and not difficult to define. It is all embraced
in the one word, independence. A man cannot talk as
he should talk with the clutch of a hand on his throat.

No more can a newspaper. The editor who must write as somebody else may dictate, who must submit his proofs to some politician for alterations or erasures, is a slave, no matter how fat an office he may fill or how plethoric a purse he may carry in his pocket. A public journal is useful and influential just in proportion as it is independent. The daily that dares not criticise a Congressman for fear of being deprived of a little government advertising, or the weekly which dares not expose the corruption of a rascally court-house ring for fear of losing the county printing, is not the kind of paper that has power or commands public respect and confidence.

THE IDOL BUSINESS.

Still weaker and no more reputable is the practice of deliberately cringing to every man in power, merely because he holds office. The true journalist never stoops to boot-licking. I know there is an old newspaper superstition still current, even in enlightened and progressive Kansas, that when a man is elected to office he somehow loses for the time the common attributes of humanity and becomes a sort of holy image, which common folks must needs approach with awe and address in prayer. This idea—and I say it with all due respect—is a pure illusion. I am sure of it, for I have seen it tested. I have known very small men to walk straight up to these terrible ghosts, time and again, and talk to them in language vigorously profane. Elphinstone relates that when Mahmoud, of Ghuznee, commenced to destroy the sumptuous temple of Somnauth, in British India, the populace besought him with cries and tears to spare the great idol of Siva therein enshrined, declaring that if it were rudely touched the very earth would open and swallow the city; but Mahmoud went on with his work, and when he pierced the mighty Siva, lo! only beans and bran fell

from his stomach—whereupon the people laughed and
shouted and burnt the punctured effigy in a bonfire.

The political idol business, in this country, is the
silliest of humbugs. When a man is chosen to office he
does not change his nature or pass beyond the range of
ordinary criticism. It is not only the right, but the duty,
of the vigilant editor to watch him, and keep the public
fully advised of his actions—to constantly hold a whip
over him, and to lash him promptly and keenly whenever he grows lazy, neglectful, tricky or corrupt.

PERSONAL RESPONSIBILITY.

But in so doing the editor should exercise care as well
as courage, and hold himself personally responsible for
what he says. In the first Kansas Legislature—sixteen
years ago—Mr. McMeekin moved that if any reporter
vilified any member, the member so vilified should be
authorized and expected to thrash him. That theory
ought to be a law in our journalism. The writer who
assumes to probe the motives and assail the conduct or
character of public men or private citizens should stand
ready at all times to make good his charges or take a
thrashing. Under such a plan, aggrieved parties could
obtain satisfaction much more surely and promptly than
they now do in libel suits, and the offending editors
would escape the expense and annoyance of attending
court.

NEWSPAPERS AND PARTIES.

Not only in personal concerns, but in party affairs
also, is independence the editor's true policy. Because a
man publishes a party paper, it does not follow that he
should endorse and support every man and measure,
however objectionable, that the party may put forward.
He is not bound to play the fawning sycophant to party
"managers," or lend his aid to the advancement of those

whom he knows or believes to be incompetent or untrustworthy. He has no right to help hide or excuse weakness or wrong for partisan purposes. His duty to the people always takes precedence to his duty to his party. And, indeed, in doing his duty to the people he performs the highest service for his party. Stereotyped approval and indiscriminate praise of everything party leaders and party conventions may do or propose, is a pleasant way to conduct a paper; but it is not the honest, the true, the best way. An editor who is content to turn the crank of a dependent party organ, playing only such tunes as the chief wire-pullers may fancy or direct, will have no influence with thinking men, and no claim upon the public for support.

In these times a newspaper can not only afford to be independent, but it can poorly afford to be anything else. Our people care more for truth and right than they do for temporary partisan advantages; and they will allow no paper to languish or fall which stands upon such a platform. God speed the day when every paper in Kansas, and throughout the country, shall be a people's paper, too proud and too prosperous for politicians to control or lead astray!

JOURNALISTIC SINCERITY.

The journalist of all men in the world should be the most sincere and straightforward, the most consistent and progressive. The dissemination of sound and true views, simple because they are sound and true, is the strength and splendor of journalism. An insincere man cannot write effectively. The editor who aims only to reflect the popular opinion of the hour will never do a community any good or himself any honor. To write and publish things that you do not yourself seriously believe is dishonest, though three-fourths of your readers may hold

the opinions you furnish. A man has no more right to
lie or dissemble in a newspaper than from the pulpit.

PUBLIC OPINION.

The widely current idea that newspapers should speak
only what is set down for them by the average judgment
of their readers is an error, and a pernicious one. Newspapers make public opinion,—or should do so. Their
mission is to be useful as well as popular—to be foremost
in explaining events, exposing wrongs, correcting mis-
takes and proclaiming new truths. Burke declared that
he consulted public opinion, indeed, and the opinion of
his constituents, but not their opinion in the immediate
present, but the opinion he believed they would have ten
or twenty years hence. Not for to-day merely, but for
to-morrow also; not simply for the next change of the
moon, but for a lifetime as well, should the faithful journalist think and feel and write.

THE OLD AND THE NEW.

To stand in Boston without blessing God for Plymouth
Rock and Bunker Hill is accounted in our National creed
a sin of the first magnitude. So should it be considered
a piece of moral treachery to speak upon any subject in
this later and fresher Boston, " the historic city " of Lawrence, without extolling the men and women who gave
to Mount Oread and Massachusetts Street

" A glory that was Greece,
A grandeur that was Rome."

Honor, then, to those who here built the first Kansas
cabins and prayed the first Kansas prayers—whose con-
stancy and courage and energy wrought the early life of
our State into an Iliad of imperishable splendor. May
their names and their services never be obscured or for-
gotten!

The "old times," however, properly belong to history.
The graves of martyrs are points to step from, and not to
stand upon. Since the "old settlers" did their work
here the world has taken a "new departure." The years
that have elapsed since Lawrence was founded make up
but a short measure of time, and yet, in that period, it
might almost be said that the whole universe has changed
front. We are face to face with facts and thoughts, with
tastes and fancies, that were not dreamed of in the
"squatter sovereign" days. New tasks have been given
us, new chances placed before us, new responsibilities
imposed upon us. The voice of Providence in the events
of the last fifteen years—events rivaling in wondrousness
the great drama of the Apocalypse itself—is an appeal
for progress, and not an invitation to repose. "Speak to
the children of Israel that they go forward" is the Divine
command to-day as clearly and distinctly as it was when
the words were first uttered.

WORK STILL AHEAD.

The conflicts of the past, fruitful as they were of good
results, accomplished but little compared with what they
made practicable to be effected. The present has its
opportunities, the future its possibilities, no less inspiring
and exalting than the best we have yet seen or studied.
The truths have not all been told, the wrongs have not
all been righted. Agitation and improvement are the
watch-words of the hour. What has been done is well,
but there is work still ahead. New economical and
political issues, new social and casuistic problems, are
waiting to be tested and solved. We cannot avoid them
if we would. They must be met. And they must be
dealt with through practical and progressive means. We
cannot fight the new battles and win the new triumphs
with the "Betsys" and "Old Sacramentos" of border-

ruffian times. Captain Bickerton's awkward old guns
were powerful in their day. And so, for that matter,
were the rams' horns at Jericho. But the dangers and
duties that now confront us require weapons of different
and improved patterns.

CONCLUSION.

Above all other things do we need a vigorous and
vigilant press—

> "Mightiest of all the mighty means
> On which the arm of Progress leans."

Nothing else will fill its place, and nothing else can stay
its force. Give us that, and the world will move, let who
or what may object or oppose. Keep journalism in full
accord and sympathy with the spirit of the age, and there
will be no going backward, and no standing still. Let
the newspapers push forward, and the people will follow,
leaving the dead past to bury its dead, as God intended
from the beginning. Strife there must be, and sometimes misfortune; but with the press in the advance—
awaking, encouraging, inciting the masses—there can be
no pause and no retreat. In this grand march to the
greater good and higher glory which the future has in
store for us, may Kansas lead the van and be first to reap
the fruits of victory.

RECORD OF PROCEEDINGS.

LAWRENCE, Oct. 24th, 1871.

The convention was called to order at 12 o'clock, M., by Vice President Murdock.

On motion of Mr. Stotler, Mr. Winter was chosen Secretary *pro. tem.*

Mr. Kalloch, chairman of the citizens' committee of reception, asked and was granted leave to make a statement concerning the arrangements of the people of Lawrence for the entertainment of the members of the convention. He invited the convention to a free ride to the State University during the afternoon and to a banquet in the evening, or to either as the convention might desire.

Mr. Stotler moved that as the convention had assembled for the transaction of important business and had but little time at its disposal, the invitation to a free ride be declined and the invitation to the banquet accepted.

Mr. Anthony moved to amend the motion so as to accept the invitation to take the ride at 4.30 o'clock, P. M.

After considerable discussion, Mr. Anthony withdrew his amendment, and Mr. Stotler's motion was carried.

On motion of Mr. Stotler, it was ordered that all members pay their dues, and that all those desirous of joining the Association sign the constitution and pay the initiation fee.

The chair read the order of business, as prepared by the committee appointed for the purpose prior to the meeting of the convention.

On motion of Mr. Stotler, the regular order of business was suspended, and the chair was authorized to appoint committees consisting of three members each on the following questions—the committees to report at the beginning of the afternoon session: Kansas Magazine, by-laws, job and press-work, advertising and general recommendations.

The chair announced the appointment of the committees as follows:

On Kansas Magazine: Wilder, King and Kalloch.

On By-Laws: Stotler, Taylor and Prescott.

On Job and Press work: Winter, Thacher and Tiernan.

On Advertising: Prescott, Brown and Martin.

On General Recommendations: Baker, MacDonald and Abbott.

Mr. Brown offered the following resolution:

Resolved, That the publishers of the State in convention assembled regard the law creating the office of State Printer as detrimental to an economical administration of our State finances, and we recommend such action as will secure a repeal of the same.

On motion of Mr. Thacher the resolution was ordered

to be referred to a special commitee of three, to be appointed by the Chair.

The Chair appointed as said committee, Messrs. Thacher, Martin and Brown.

On motion of Mr. Prescott, the same committee was directed to consider and report upon the question of the expediency of amending or abolishing the law passed by the State Legislature at its last session creating a State Insurance Department.

On motion of Mr. Stotler, the convention adjourned to meet again at 3 o'clock, P. M.

AFTERNOON SESSION.

The convention re-assembled at 3 o'clock P. M., President Reynolds in the chair.

Mr. Stotler, chairman of the committee on by-laws, read the following report:

Your committee would recommend that section No. 2 of the By-Laws of the Association be so amended as to read as follows:

SEC. 2. The president and secretary of this association shall call the annual meeting at such place as they may designate, or as may be decided at a previous annual meeting, some time during the month of June of each year.

The report was adopted and the committee discharged.

Mr. Wilder, chairman of the committee on Kansas Magazine, submitted the following report:

Your committee to whom was referred the project of establishing a monthly literary magazine in Kansas beg leave to report that they have had the matter under consideration and would recommend the adoption by the convention of the following preamble and resolutions:

WHEREAS, The project of establishing in Kansas a

literary magazine, similar in style and purpose to the *Overland Monthly*, and other publications of that character, has been proposed and discussed by the press of the State, and formally brought to the attention of this Association:

Therefore, Be it resolved, That this Association views said enterprise with favor and confidence, and hereby pledges it the fullest encouragement, assistance and support.

2. *Resolved,* That the president of this Association be and he is hereby empowered and instructed to appoint a committee of three members of the Association to take the whole matter in charge, and in such way as shall seem to them best and most expedient, begin and carry on the publication of the proposed magazine.

3. *Resolved,* That said magazine shall be a Kansas magazine, in fact as well as in name, devoting a liberal share of its space to State history and State characteristics, and giving preference at all times to contributions from Kansas writers.

4. *Resolved,* That the mechanical work upon said magazine shall be the best that can be done in the State, and of a character to favorably compare with the leading magazines of the country.

5. *Resolved,* That the literary men and women of the State be requested to furnish said magazine with contributions and generally to lend it all the aid in their power.

6. *Resolved,* That this Association earnestly commends said magazine to the attention of the people of the State and country, and solicits for it a fair share of public patronage, at home and abroad.

7. *Resolved,* That the newspapers of Kansas be requested to gratuitously advertise said magazine in such form and to such extent as its conductors may desire, and to give it such editorial commendation, from time to time, as it may appear to merit.

8. *Resolved,* That the committee hereinbefore authorized shall have full control of the magazine, with power to select an editor and publisher, to fix prices for subscriptions and advertising, to make all contracts, and to receive and disburse all funds—a complete report of which they shall submit to this Association at each of its annual meetings.

9. *Resolved,* That the president, first vice president

and secretary of this Association be and they are hereby
constituted an advisory committee to co-operate with
the magazine committee in such ways and on such points
as said magazine committee may signify.

The report was adopted, and the President appointed
the following-named members as the committee to take
charge of the magazine enterprise: Messrs. Wilder,
King and Prouty.

Mr. Winter, chairman of the committee on job and
press work, made the following report:

Mr President: As chairman of the committee on
job and press work I would report that the committee
deem it unwise to take any step in regard to the scale of
prices of the above work as recommended in the circular.

After remarks by several members, Mr. Crowther
moved that the matter be referred back to the committee
with instructions to recommend a scale of prices, and
that the committee be increased from three to seven
members. The motion was carried.

The President announced the following-named gentlemen as additional members of the committee: Messrs.
Crowther, Nelson and M. M. Murdock.

On motion the following-named members were appointed a committee to recommend officers for the ensuing year, with instructions to report at the evening session: Messrs. Baker, Warner, Martin, Anthony and
Claridy.

Mr. Prescott, chairman of the committee on advertisements, made a report recommending the adoption of the
following scale of prices:

For weekly papers, $1.00 per inch, per month, net.

For daily papers, the following scale :

NUMBER OF TIMES.	1 Square.	2 Squares.	3 Squares.	1/8 Column.	1/4 Column.	1/2 Column.	1 Column.
1 Insertion	$1 00	$1 50	$2 00	$3 00	$6 00	$10 00	$15 00
Additions	50	75	1 00	1 00	3 00	8 00	5 00
1 Week	8 00	5 00	6 00	7 00	10 00	15 00	25 00
2 Weeks	4 50	6 00	7 00	9 00	15 00	20 00	30 00
3 Weeks	5 50	7 50	9 00	12 00	20 00	30 00	35 00
1 Month	6 00	8 00	12 00	15 00	25 00	35 00	40 00
2 Months	9 00	12 00	15 80	25 00	35 00	50 00	75 00
3 Months	12 00	15 00	25 00	35 00	50 00	75 00	100 00
6 Months	20 00	25 00	35 00	50 00	75 00	100 00	150 00
1 Year	31 00	40 00	55 00	75 00	100 00	150 00	250 00

For both daily and weekly edition, a price and a half.
Legal advertisements, legal rates on all occasions.

The same committee also submitted the following recommendations, which were adopted :

We recommend that the law by which county printing is let to the lowest bidder, be so amended as to leave it to the County Board to give to such local paper as they shall choose at legal rates; and that all county and city printing, and book binding, be required to be done in the State.

No member of this association shall bid for county, city, or other public work, at less rates than are established by law.

We recommend the passage of a resolution asking all political caucuses and conventions to raise money to pay the necessary expenses of advertising calls for conventions and other political advertisements, and the necessary printing to conduct a canvass, and that hereafter the members of this association will do no work of that kind without some responsible person becomes security for the payment thereof.

We recommend that the convention pass a resolution denouncing the publication, without pay, of any and all notices for Churches, Societies, Festivals, etc., and that the members hereafter refuse to do so without receiving one-half regular rates.

We recommend that the subscription price of weekly papers shall not be less than $2.00 per year. That the price of daily papers shall be $10.00 per year.

Mr. Baker moved that the report be adopted. A lengthy discussion ensued, and, at a late hour, the consideration of the subject was, on motion, postponed until to-morrow morning.

On motion of Mr. Taylor the convention adjourned until 7:30 o'clock P. M.

The convention met at 7:30 o'clock, P. M., President Reynolds in the chair.

The President introduced Capt. Henry King, who delivered the annual address.

At the conclusion of the address, Mr. Burlingame moved that the thanks of the convention be tendered to Capt. King for his able and entertaining address, and that one thousand copies of the address be printed at the expense of the Association. The motion was carried.

The committee on nominations asked for further time, and was, on motion, directed to report to-morrow morning.

On motion of Mr. Baker, the convention adjourned to meet at 8:30 o'clock, A. M. to-morrow.

Wednesday, Oct. 25th, 1871.

The convention met at 8:30 o'clock, A. M., President Reynolds in the chair.

The committee on nominations reported the following as officers for the ensuing year, and the report was adopted and the nominees elected by the convention ;

For President: M. W. Reynolds.

For Vice Presidents: G. F. Prescott, D. W. Wilder,
Geo. C. Crowther and Albert Griffin.

For Secretary: S. D. Macdonald.

For Treasurer: S. S. Prouty.

On motion, Geo. A. Crawford was chosen to deliver
the next annual address, and D. W. Wilder was selected
as alternate.

The committee on State printing and insurance law,
submitted the following report, which was adopted:

Your committee, to whom was referred the matter of
State printing and the repeal of the insurance law, would
respectfully report that, in their opinion, the change in
the constitution, providing for a State printing house,
bindery and State paper, introduces elements of unfair
competition with the other publishers and printers in
the State, that has resulted in greatly increased expenditures for printing purposes; and that the law providing
for a State paper should be repealed, to take effect July
1, 1873, and the binding should be let to the lowest
bidder.

As to the repeal of the old insurance law, we would
report that we believe the same to have been unnecessary
and unwise, and that the law should be restored, substantially as it stood before.

T. D. THACHER,
A. D. BROWN,
JNO. A. MARTIN.

Mr. Elliott offered the following resolution:

Resolved, That a committee of three be appointed to
correspond with the publishers of the papers of Kansas,
to ascertain what amount of paper is used in the State
per annum, and then to correspond with paper makers,
and endeavor to induce some one to establish a paper
manufactory in the State.

The resolution was adopted, and the chair appointed
as the committee Mr. Elliott, T. B. Murdock and Geo.
A. Crawford.

Mr. Griffin, of Manhattan, offered the following resolution:

Resolved, That a committee of three be appointed by the chair to correspond with publishers, type founders and paper makers, for the purpose of ascertaining if something cannot be done to secure greater uniformity in the size of cases and of type of the same nominal size. Also, to have the number of sheets in a quire of paper reduced to twenty, with twenty-five quires to a ream, and to inaugurate other similar reforms.

On motion, the resolution was adopted, and the chair appointed Messrs. Griffin, Jones and Good the committee.

Mr. Crowther was authorized to collect the amount due the association from P. H. Peters, the defaulting Treasurer, and to take legal steps if necessary.

The committee on general recommendations submitted the following report:

Your committee, to whom was referred the general recommendations of the Topeka committee, have attended to that duty and find that the following portions of that report have not heretofore been referred to any committee:

We recommend that the convention advise that associations be formed in all places where more than one paper is published, and that they shall agree upon rates for all kinds of local advertising, and that they be kept up to as near the prices fixed by this convention as possible.

In order to effect the proposed changes in the laws, and others we hereafter submit, we recommend that the convention appoint a committee of at least three persons, to have charge of the interests of publishers during the next and each succeeding session of the Legislature. It shall be the duty of such committee to try and secure an amendment to the law by which the State furnishes all blanks free to school districts; by which estrays are published in but one paper in the State; and by which the

Educational Journal is sent free to each school district in the State.

We recommend that the Legislature direct the county clerks of each county to subscribe for and keep on file every paper published in the county, and at the close of a volume, to have the same bound.

We recommend that the Secretary be instructed immediately after the close of the convention, to cause to be published the Constitution and By-Laws, rates of advertising, etc., and send to all publishers in the State, not already members of the Association, with a request that they sign the same and return it to the Secretary. It also should be his duty, when a paper is started in the State, to send the publisher a copy of the Constitution and By-Laws, and induce him, or them, if possible, to become members of the Association.

We recommend that this Association agree to the above.

F. P. BAKER,
NELSON ABBOTT.

I concur in the foregoing with the exception of the recommendation about the estray list and *Educational Journal.*

S. S. PROUTY.

On motion the report was accepted and the president appointed the following-named gentlemen to constitute the committee: Messrs. King, Crowther, Davis, Stotler and M. M. Murdock.

Mr. Crawford offered the following resolution, which was adopted:

Resolved, That the committee to whom was referred the recommendation asking the Legislature to repeal or amend the insurance law, be also instructed to endeavor to get a change in the law relating to State printing, providing for the election of a State Printer or Superintendent, and that the printing and binding be hereafter done by contract, under the supervision of the printer elected by the Legislature.

Mr. Martin submitted the following resolution, which was adopted:

Resolved, That no person shall be eligible to membership in this Association unless he be permanently and regularly connected with one of the regularly published journals of the State, either as editor or publisher.

Mr. Anthony offered the following resolution, which was adopted:

Resolved, That the publishers of this State hereby pledge themselves not to send a paper to any subscriber or other person without payment in advance.

Mr. Winter, from the committee on press and job-work, made a report recommending substantially the scale of prices contained in the circular to the Kansas Editorial and Publishers' Association, October 1st, 1871.

On motion Emporia was selected as the place for holding the next convention, and June, 1872, as the month—the day to be selected and announced by the President and Secretary.

On motion adjourned, *sine die.*

M. W. REYNOLDS, PRESIDENT.

S. D. MACDONALD, *Secretary.*

CONSTITUTION AND BY-LAWS.

In order that it may be known just what our present organization is, we give the Constitution and By-Laws now in force.

CONSTITUTION.

ART. 1. This body shall be known as the Kansas Editorial and Publishers' Association.

ART. 2. The object of this Association is to promote the mutual welfare of the Kansas press, protect it in its rights, inculcate feelings of harmony, and elevate its tone and character.

ART. 3. The officers of this Association shall consist of a President, four Vice Presidents, Secretary, Treasurer, and an Executive Board, to consist of the President and Vice Presidents.

ART. 4. The duty of the President shall be to preside over all meetings and to maintain order.

ART. 5. Any Vice President present shall preside in the absence af the President.

ART. 6. The duties of the Secretary shall be to record the proceedings of all meetings, and read the same at each successive meeting, keep a roll of the members of the Association, to collect all dues and deposit the same with the Treasurer. He shall conduct the correspondence of the Association, file carefully all charges made against members of this Association for violation of its rules, and report all charges to the President and Vice Presidents, as soon as received.

ART. 7. The Treasurer shall receive all moneys of the Association, and pay the same out, on orders drawn by the Secretary and endorsed by the President. He shall keep a faithful record of all moneys by him received and paid out, and make an annual exhibit of the financial condition of the Association.

ART. 8. The duty of the Executive Board shall be to investigate all charges made against members reported to them by the Secretary, and they are empowered to decide cases, and impose the penalties for any violation of the rules of this Association, if, in their discretion, its interests demand summary action. The President shall report all proceedings of the Executive Board to the annual meetings of the Association, for its approval or rejection.

ART. 9. The Constitution and By-Laws of this Association shall be subject to amendment at each annual meeting, a majority of the members present concurring therein.

BY-LAWS.

SEC. 1. All editors and publishers of newspapers and periodicals, in Kansas, may become members of this Association by signing the Constitution and by the payment of **two** dollars.

SEC. 2. The President and Secretary of this Association shall call the annual meeting at such place as they may designate, or as may be decided at a previous annual meeting, some time during the month of June of each year.

SEC. 3. A quorum shall consist of a majority of the members present at any meeting.

SEC 4. The President shall have power to call a special meeting at any time, upon request of six members, and shall give notice of the same in all the newspapers of the State.

SEC. 5. The term of office for all the officers, shall be for one year, or until the annual meeting next succeeding their appointment, or until their successors shall be qualified.

SEC. 6. The Executive Board shall fill all vacancies in the offices of the Association, and shall have power to remove all officers who fail to act, or who shall violate any rules of the Association.

SEC. 7. The officers of this Association shall be elected at every annual meeting, by ballot.

SEC. 8. No member of this Association shall publish county or legal advertisements below the rates established by law. But members shall not be bound by this rule when thrown in competition with publishers not members of the Association.

SEC. 9. The Secretary shall notify all agencies within his knowledge of the existence of this Association, and the President of the Executive Board shall give immediate notice to all members of this Association, of any knowledge he may receive, affecting the responsibility of any advertising agent.

SEC. 10. Any member who shall be found guilty of violating any rule of this Association shall be subjected to such penalty as the Executive Board may deem fit.